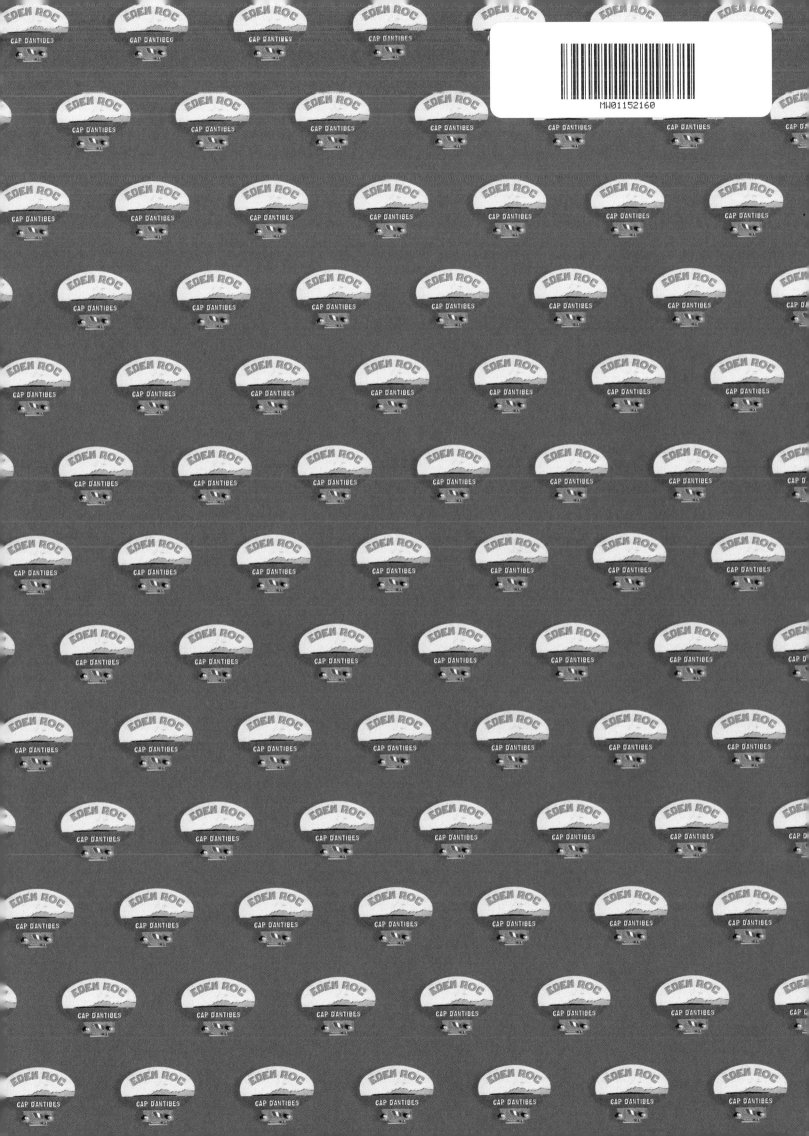

HOTEL DU CAP-EDEN-ROC
CAP D'ANTIBES

THE ARTISANS
OF
PARADISE

© 2009 Assouline Publishing
601 West 26th Street, 18th floor
New York, NY 10001 USA
Tel.: 212 989-6810   Fax: 212 647-0005
www.assouline.com

Translated from the French by Barbara Mellor
All photos by Jean-Michel Sordello,
except for page 4: © Assouline.

ISBN: 978 2 7594 03981

Color separation: Planète Couleurs (France)
Printed by Grafiche Milani (Italy)

HOTEL DU CAP - EDEN - ROC
CAP D'ANTIBES

THE ARTISANS
OF
PARADISE

Foreword by Philippe Perd

Texts by François Simon

Photographs by Jean-Michel Sordello

ASSOULINE

Preface

I remember that magical moment on the terrace of the Hôtel du Cap Eden-Roc, looking out over the Mediterranean. I was trying to think of a description that would do justice to the men and women I see working here so conscientiously, day after day, toiling away in the background and spinning dreams, when François Simon, one of the hotel's most fervent admirers, remarked: "They are the artisans of paradise!"

We had hit upon the title of this new volume, the culmination of a timely trilogy and a heartfelt tribute to those who work behind the scenes in this legendary hotel that I never —not for a single day—tire of serving.

Having traced the legends of this iconic spot in the first volume and honored the culinary talents of our chefs in the second, our attention naturally turns to those familiar faces who are the (sometimes unsung) architects of excellence; those people without whom the Hôtel du Cap Eden-Roc would be no more than a beautiful setting with no soul.

This depthless fund of goodwill, this great wealth of talents and expert hands, this multitude and diversity of specialized skills, all bound together by a feeling of belonging to one big family—this was the inspiration for this book.

From the head gardener to the handyman, via the florist, printer, painters, upholsterers, gilders, concierges and receptionists—not to mention the cavalcade of local suppliers, the market gardeners, fishermen, wine growers, coffee roasters and olive oil producers who all bring their magic to Arnaud Poëtte's kitchens—everyone makes a unique contribution.

These are the artisans of paradise, artists above all in their consummate attention to detail, always striving for even greater excellence, always giving their best. Highly skilled at anticipating the needs of a major establishment of which they know every nook and cranny, they remain constantly attentive to the requirements of a prestigious clientele with whom many of them, veterans of thirty years' service or more, have forged a bonds of special camaraderie.

May these pages steeped in passion be an expression of the gratitude that they deserve for their faithful contribution to *la belle histoire* of the Hôtel du Cap Eden-Roc.

PHILIPPE PERD
Directeur Général

Contents

Opposite: The south-facing terrace of the Hôtel du Cap, where breakfast is served.
Following pages: Yann Jule, valet.

Introduction

The thing that strikes you most forcibly as you stand on the terrace outside the Hôtel du Cap Eden-Roc is not so much its legendary bustle of activity, nor the inspiration of its heroic characters, nor the high notes of its galaxy of stars. No, it is not any of these—it is the silence. This is a silence stitched with gold and studded with attentions. Listen carefully and you may make out the muted sounds of a quiet army, creeping on tiptoe and holding their fingers to their lips. If they could have their way, the ringing of hammers would be muffled with felt and car tires would wear slippers to stifle their noise. Hiding in the shadows, slipping through the half-light, they glide down corridors and through concealed doorways as though on wings. These hushed creatures are the artisans of paradise. Rarely will you hear any signs of their presence, except, perhaps, for the voice of the receptionist. Light tones and morning cheerfulness only —the tessitura of linen, a greeting like silk. The life of a luxury hotel, you begin to realize, its great talent and its strength, lies in fact with the accumulation of a mass of apparently insignificant details. All the difference rests in the single-minded, unwavering way in which those details are assembled. Where other establishments may lose heart and give up, the Hôtel du Cap Eden-Roc persists undaunted. It insists on paying attention to all those tiny details and services, and above all, in desiring only the best for those who have chosen to stay in this paradise—its treasured guests. Those who stay at other luxury hotels may be "clients." Not here. You only have to spend a few minutes at the Reception to realize that those who choose to come here do so above all in order not to be treated as clients. For that is how their lives are spent, and now and then it is a misunderstanding of which they grow weary, dismayed at being held at arm's length by the language of commerce. What they really want is to step down from

Opposite: A family photograph taken on October 18, 2008.

Above: A business meeting between Philippe Perd, Managing Director (center),
and Laurent Vanhoegaerden, Resident Manager (left).

their clouds, to be greeted by their first names. For someone to ask after their children, their dogs, their houses, their lives, to remark how well they look, to inquire how their tennis lesson went. Someone who might even put an arm around them and give them a comforting embrace. Between the Hôtel du Cap Eden-Roc and its loyal staff there exists a pact of natural simplicity and common sense; there is a bond of something approaching fond camaraderie between those who have chosen to stay here and those who work here. These, then, are the artisans of paradise, generally believed to be anonymous but rarely remaining so for long. For when the sheets on the bed are sleek as marble, one cannot help but imagine the expert hands that smoothed out the creases. When the rose blooms are so perfect, one's thoughts turn to the hands that pruned and tended the bushes. Every moment here is honed by someone's skills and talents:

Above: *Philippe Perd (left) and Laurent Vanhoegaerden.*

The chef who adds the final swirl of sauce, the pastry chef who dusts his delectable creation with confectioner's sugar, the sommelier who refills the carafe and glasses, the waiter who wheels his tray between the tables, the doorman who parks your car with such aplomb, the pool man who unfurls your umbrella, the linen maid who ensures that your gown hangs perfectly . . . Take a little trouble one day to note these invisible attentions, these tiny gestures that make up paradise. Not a moment of time, not an inch of space is overlooked: A dead leaf, scratched paint, a missing coaster or magazine, a missed flight, a shirt to be ironed, another cappuccino—everything seems to be anticipated, perhaps because they know you better here than anywhere else. While you sleep, the artisans of paradise carry on working. The strawberry grower, for one, threads her way through the dawn mists, inspecting the fruit with her expert eye, deftly

picking the ripe berries and putting them in crates before setting off in her van for the hotel kitchens. Later, when you call room service, the grapefruit you prefer for breakfast will arrive, accompanied by toast (prepared just as you like it, of course), the newspapers—and strawberries still bathed in their morning freshness. In these pages, Jean-Michel Sordello has followed these artisans of paradise with his camera. In the weeks he spent with them, he discovered the tireless work that goes into the constant tending of this little heaven on earth. His photographs are accompanied by the words of the painstaking workforce that creates this idyllic refuge, reflecting on their work, what they love most about it, their proudest skill, what they wear . . . If their words sometimes have the ring of another age, this is because the Hôtel du Cap Eden-Roc is one of those venerable institutions where "respect," "high standards," "passion," and "commitment" are still common currency. These pages bear witness to a possibility that has all but vanished in today's world: A return trip to paradise.

Opposite: A group photograph of the hotel staff in 1954, taken in celebration of the presentation of the Légion d'Honneur to the director, André Sella.

The Staff

———◆◆◆———

Life is full of ups and downs,
as the lift attendant used to say.

ALPHONSE ALLAIS, Journal

Opposite: *Antonio Marques, valet.*

THE DOORMAN
Philippe Madar

For more than twenty-one years, Philippe has scanned the horizon, ever on the alert. When you first arrive, he will be there to greet you, to open the car door for you, and take care of your luggage. After the Head of Reception, Philippe will be among the first people you encounter at the Hôtel du Cap Eden-Roc.

Tell us an anecdote: During the Cannes Film Festival one year, a bodyguard asked me if I would take his lady guest for a ride in the gardens. She sat next to me in the golf buggy, and we chatted away very happily. After an hour in her charming company, I was still puzzling over the identity of this pretty young woman. As we rode around, guests would stop us in order to take her photograph, and she would comply with great good humor. After she had gone, I asked her bodyguard who she was. "Do you mean to say you didn't recognize her?" he asked. "That was Kylie Minogue!" But then, she didn't recognize me, either.

The best part about your job: Dealing with guests, and belonging to what feels in a way like one big family.

The hardest part about your job: Coping with the unexpected, and with the heat in high summer.

The skill that encapsulates your professionalism: Opening a car door with elegance, carrying a bag with style.

The tool you can't do without: The telephone.

The sound that tells you all is well: The chirping of the cicadas.

Your favorite time or place: Morning coffee in the dining room.

What do you wear for work? Beige suit, blue tie.

Would you like to have done a different job? Why not? But it would have to be working with people.

Your most memorable experience with a guest: The day when I passed Bill Cosby out running and brought him back to the hotel on my scooter.

A gift you like to give: Flowers.

YOUR MOTTO:

"Experience is not so much what happens to you as what you do with what happens to you."

Opposite: *Philippe Madar (left) and Marc Pages, doormen.*

THE CHIEF CONCIERGE
Gilles Bertolino

If the discreet warmth and efficiency of the personnel forms the soothing soundtrack to every stay at the Hôtel du Cap Eden-Roc, the opening notes of the melody are sounded by the concierge team. For over twenty years, Gilles has provided the expert accompaniment to the subtle cadences of this chamber music.

Tell us an anecdote: My managing director gave me the sack on my first day. That was twenty-three years ago now!

The best thing about your job: Meeting people.

The hardest thing about your job: The lack of time.

The skill that encapsulates your professionalism: Smiling.

The tool you can't do without: My team.

The sound that tells you all is well: Laughter.

What do you wear for work? My uniform.

Would you have liked to do something different? No.

Your most memorable experience with a guest: The complete trust guests put in me.

A gift you like to give: My time and services.

YOUR MOTTO:

"Keep smiling."

Opposite: Gilles Bertolino, chief concierge (left), and Thierry Dupray, his deputy.

THE FRONT DESK MANAGER
Jean-Jacques Socquet-Juglard

Jean-Jacques has been in charge of reception at the Hôtel du Cap since 1981. He is the one who will greet you on your arrival, the one who will set the tone for entire your stay. He has the delicate responsibility of ushering guests inside, a ritual requiring discretion and efficiency in equal measures.

The best part about your job: Guests' discretion and loyalty.

The hardest part about your job: The demanding pace that never stops.

The skill that encapsulates your professionalism: I am very particular about writing with care; for me, handwriting sums up the elegance of my work.

The tool you can't do without: The ability to speak well: the tone, the rhythm, and the clarity of my voice should inspire confidence in guests. The voice says it all.

The sound that tells you all is well: Paradoxically, silence.

The most frustrating thing: Failure to give satisfaction.

Your favorite time or place: The perron staircase leading down to the gardens at sunset.

What do you wear for work? Blazer and tie.

A gift you like to give: Chocolates.

YOUR MOTTO:

"I will maintain."

THE RECEPTIONIST
Pascale Bianchi

For seven years now, Pascale's smile has been the first sight to greet you at Reception in the Hôtel du Cap Eden-Roc, the first note in the opening bars of the symphony you are about to experience. . .

Tell us an anecdote: I was once rather reluctant to take an actor up to his room, as he was notorious for his performance as a bad boy in a very popular movie. Nothing could have been further from the truth!

The best part about your job: The contact with guests, my colleagues, the perfectionism, the rigor and the professionalism.

The hardest part about your job: The unrelenting rhythm of my work, and the need to satisfy the expectations and requirements of our guests.

The skill that encapsulates your professionalism: Guess! My smile.

The tool you can't do without: The telephone.

The sound that tells you all is well: The chirping of the cicadas.

The most frustrating thing: The rain!

Your favorite time or place: Mealtimes in the canteen.

What do you wear for work? A navy blue suit.

Would you like to have done a different job? Yes, I would have liked to have been a psychologist.

Your most memorable experience with a guest: The day Bruce Willis flashed his smile at me—devastating!

A gift you like to give: Whatever gives the recipient the most pleasure.

YOUR MOTTO:

"Passion in everything."

Opposite: *Laurent Vaunaize (left) and Frédéric Debord, concierges.*

THE HOUSEKEEPER
Marie-Claire Vary

Since May 1992 Marie-Claire has patrolled the length and breadth of the corridors of the Hôtel du Cap Eden-Roc. Whatever you need—be it a recalcitrant suitcase, a creased shirt, or an extra feather pillow—Marie-Claire will be there to help you. While you lounge beside the pool, she and her team will ensure that everything in your room is immaculate. Not a speck of dust, not the slightest detail out of place, escapes the eagle eye of Marie-Claire.

Tell us an anecdote: We embroidered all of one guest's linen with his initials so that every time he returned he would have his own linen.

The best part about your job: The punctuality, conscientiousness, and contact with guests.

The hardest part about your job: The attention to detail needed to achieve the highest standards.

The skill that encapsulates your professionalism: Checking a forgotten corner for that last speck of dust.

The tool you can't do without: There are so many: Keys, telephone, duster . . .

Your favorite time or place: The general housekeepers' office, for planning meetings and daily reports.

What do you wear for work? A suit.

Would you like to have done a different job? No, I love my work.

A gift you like to give: Flowers.

YOUR MOTTO:

"Achievement."

Opposite: Christiane Champclaux, floor attendant.
Following pages: Béatrice Caddeo, floor attendant.

THE ROOM SERVICE MANAGER, HÔTEL DU CAP

Georges Renaldi

In charge of room service at the Hôtel du Cap since 1974, Georges is the discreet and efficient witness to the two parallel universes that unfold behind the scenes in the hotel and exist outside in the sunshine. His lips are sealed . . . almost . . .

Tell us an anecdote: During my first season here, when I was just starting in the business, I was fortunate enough to serve the great soccer star Pelé! A stroke of magic was transformed into true happiness when he congratulated me and offered me a Coke. This was just the beginning of a long, star-studded line of heads of state and performing artists.

The best part about your job: Making arrangements for guests.

The hardest part about your job: Ensuring we all work to the highest standards.

The skill that encapsulates your professionalism: Unobtrusive discretion in service and presentation.

The tool you can't do without: A smile.

The sound that tells you all is well: Silence.

Your favorite time or place: At home with my wife and children.

What do you wear for work? Clothing that reflects my personality.

Would you like to have done a different job? No.

Your most memorable experience with a guest: Marc Chagall once inscribed a book for me —despite being reluctant to sign the hotel bill.

A gift you like to give: Flowers.

YOUR MOTTO:

"Respect."

THE ROOM SERVICE MANAGER, EDEN-ROC PAVILION
Michel Giraud

Michel has been head of room service since April 1, 1990. As maître d'hôtel, he is constantly waiting in the wings. Press the button on your telephone, and Michel will answer instantly, greeting you by name and listening attentively to your smallest whim. Whether you would like breakfast, an aspirin or your hometown paper, Michel will strive to meet your every need.

Tell us an anecdote: There are so many! Never a day passes without something unexpected happening. I remember being chased down the corridors and pelted with potato puree by a famous journalist after an argument about soccer. In the end we made up and had a good laugh about it.

The best part about your job: Relations with guests, and the pleasure of making them happy.

The hardest part about your job: Saying no to a guest while at the same time offering an alternative solution that will keep him happy.

The skill that encapsulates your professionalism: There is only one: The ability to keep smiling.

The tool you can't do without: A mobile phone.

The sound that tells you all is well: Silence.

The most frustrating thing: The unpredictability of the weather.

Your most memorable experience with a guest: The time when, after I'd served breakfast, someone led me by the hand through the suite in total darkness, talking to me softly. That someone was Madonna.

YOUR MOTTO:
"Organization, anticipation, and diplomacy
—but most of all, perpetual good humor!"

Opposite: Didier Valette, chef de rang

THE LAUNDRYMAN
Patrick Paoli

You are unlikely to encounter Patrick during your stay; for eight years he has worked behind the scenes amongst the washing machines. You may not see him but you will experience his work in the clean, fresh scent of your sheets. He works in the annex on the left as you arrive at the Hôtel du Cap Eden-Roc.

Tell us an anecdote: The time I forgot to put in the laundry detergent—silly but annoying.

The best part about your job: You're your own boss. You have the day ahead of you, and you know exactly what's to be done. You don't need anyone to tell you.

The hardest part about your job: Loading and emptying the machines.

The skill that encapsulates your professionalism: The way I handle the linen and especially the weight of the trolleys.

The tool you can't do without: Laundry detergent.

The sound that tells you all is well: The noise of the machines—though it's not great for your ears!

The most frustrating thing: Stains.

What do you wear for work? Shorts and T-shirt.

Would you like to have done a different job? Yes, a croupier.

YOUR MOTTO:

"As long as you have your health, you can work."

Opposite: Berreguane Bekkay, the laundryman.
Following pages: Khadija Gressard, linen maid;
right: Patrick Agnese, valet.

THE EXECUTIVE HOUSEKEEPER
Marie-Christine Saison

There is something exhilarating about overseeing the housekeeping of the hotel and ensuring that it runs smoothly, from the smallest details to the overall harmony of a room. You need to keep your eyes and ears open, to check and double-check. Looking after the hotel means never stopping: This has been Marie-Christine's daily routine for some twenty years.

Tell us an anecdote: A guest once informed us that he was going to propose marriage to his companion and asked us to scatter the room with a carpet of rose petals.

The best part about your job: Dealing with guests and staff, the variety of things to be done and the daily challenges.

The hardest part about your job: Getting the best out of people while maintaining a good relationship with them. The demands of a job well done.

The skill that encapsulates your professionalism: Casting that last glance over a finished job.

The tool you can't do without: Keys, telephone, toothbrush, screwdriver.

Your favorite time or place: The housekeepers' office, for planning meetings and weekly reports.

What do you wear for work? A suit.

Would you like to have done a different job? No.

A gift you like to give: Books.

YOUR MOTTO:

"Onward and upward."

Preceding pages: *(from left to right) Marianna Lanzetta, Aurelia Da Silva, Halima Hamdan and Consuela Biondo, linen attendants.*
Opposite: *Marie-Christine Saison, executive housekeeper, and Marie-Claire Vary, housekeeper.*

THE HEAD LINEN ATTENDANT
AND SEAMSTRESS
Consuela Biondo

In the world of the Eden-Roc, the ironing room is the scene of some of the most concentrated and fastidious attention to detail. In this realm of razor-sharp pleats and porcelain-smooth cuffs and collars, Consuela and her team stitch and press the very finest of fabrics.

The best part about your job: Working with luxury fabrics.

The hardest part about your job: Putting bias-cut tablecloths through the steam press without losing their shape.

The skill that encapsulates your professionalism: Taking accurate measurements.

The tool you can't do without: A thimble.

The sound that tells you all is well: The hum of the sewing machines.

The most frustrating thing: The radio.

Your favorite time or place: The friendly atmosphere when the whole team stops for a tea or coffee break.

What do you wear for work? A white coat.

Would you like to have done a different job? No.

Your most memorable experience with a guest: Whenever a guest wears a garment that you have just altered and it hangs perfectly.

A gift you like to give: Flowers.

YOUR MOTTO:

"Treat your work with respect."

THE HEAD IRONING ATTENDANT
Andrée Berillion

Having worked at the Hôtel du Cap Eden-Roc for twenty-five years, Andrée is familiar with the innermost secrets of its comforts for it is she who smooths your bed linen and provides the perfectly folded towels for your bathroom. All this behind-the-scenes work takes place a short distance from the hotel, in the annex to your left as you enter the grounds.

Tell us an anecdote: One day when there was a big wedding with lots of evening gowns, we were under so much pressure that all of a sudden we felt completely overwhelmed. It doesn't often happen, but when it does, it's really stressful!

The best part about your job: Ironing our guests' beautiful linens.

The hardest part about your job: Some of the evening gowns.

Joséphine Guirre (left) and Élisabeth Clémente (right), ironing attendants.

The skill that encapsulates your professionalism: Ironing silk and chiffon.

The tool you can't do without: My iron is my constant work companion.

The sound that tells you all is well: The humming of the irons.

Your favorite time or place: My workshop.

What do you wear for work? A white coat.

Your most memorable experience with a guest: The most beautiful wedding gown—it made me feel as though I'd been invited to the wedding!

A gift you like to give: Flowers.

YOUR MOTTO:

"Good organization is half the job done."

THE HEAD LINEN ATTENDANT
AND SEAMSTRESS
Angèle Rocher

For nearly seven years, Angèle has worked in a world of whiteness and softness, a world where spots and creases are banished in a quest for a better, smoother world. It's the sort of work that must be infectious, you feel.

The best part about your job: Working as a team.

The hardest part about your job: The trickiest thing, sometimes, is overseeing the organization of a team without letting the pressure get to you. You have to be able to keep calm.

The skill that encapsulates your professionalism: I'm fascinated by the quest for perfect linen.

The tool you can't do without: The ironing press.

The sound that tells you all is well: The hum of the machinery.

The most frustrating thing: Not surprisingly, stubborn stains.

Your favorite time or place: Break times!

What do you wear for work? A white coat.

Would you like to have done a different job? Yes, a hairdresser.

A gift you like to give: Perfume.

YOUR MOTTO:

"Where there's a will, there's a way."

THE WELLNESS SPA MANAGER
Valérie Dalmayrac

Nowhere at the Hôtel du Cap Eden-Roc is more serene than the Wellness Spa. Here, just behind the tennis courts, life relaxes, breathes deeply and surrenders to a shoulder massage. During nearly four years at the spa – where luxuriating to sensual delights is a virtue –Valérie has perfected the art of stretching time, of embracing tranquility.

Tell us an anecdote: Not so long ago, a guest dozed off after a treatment. He fell into such a sound sleep that it took us a while to wake him up again …

The best thing about your job: Working as a team.

The hardest thing about your job: Leaving this magical spot at the end of every season.

The skill that encapsulates your professionalism: The first touch of my hands on a guest's body, through silk sheets, then pouring warm oil on their skin.

The tool you can't do without: My hands.

The sound that tells you all is well: The slowing of a heartbeat.

The most frustrating thing: The clock.

Your favourite time or place: The rotunda by the rose garden.

What do you wear for work? White trousers and linen shirt.

Would you have liked to do something different? No.

Your most memorable experience with a guest: An unaccustomed view of the Hôtel du Cap from a guest's yacht at sea. The sunset was magnificent.

A gift you like to give: A CD.

YOUR MOTTO:

"Our hands are the extensions of our hearts."

THE POOL MAN
Jean-Luc Maïorana

You might think that a pool man's duties consist solely of wearing sunglasses and checking the angle of the umbrellas. But of course it's a good deal more complicated than that. Since he started in 1991, in fact, Jean-Luc has hardly stopped. Even on rainy days he has to put away the equipment—and his sunglasses.

Tell us an anecdote: Once a guest who was swimming in the sea was evidently in serious trouble. I managed to bring him ashore, and as I brought him up the beach, all the guests who were watching gave me a spontaneous round of applause! That's a day I'll never forget.

The best part about your job: Dealing with guests, the idyllic setting of the Hôtel du Cap Eden-Roc, the ambience.

The hardest part about your job: Demanding guests.

The skill that encapsulates your professionalism: A handshake from a guest to thank me for giving good service and for keeping their place.

The tool you can't do without: My two coworkers are the deck chair and the umbrella.

The sound that tells you all is well: Laughter.

The most frustrating thing: The weather is always in charge.

Your favorite time or place: Sun and sea.

What do you wear for work? Shorts and polo shirt.

Would you like to have done a different job? No.

Your most memorable experience with a guest: A guest invited my wife and I to dinner to thank me for my services.

A gift you like to give: Jewelry.

YOUR MOTTO:
"The early bird catches the worm
– *chi dorme non prende pesce.*"

THE MAÎTRE D'HÔTEL,
LES CABANES
Giovanni Rizzi

For more than thirty years, Giovanni has reigned over the heart of the Hôtel du Cap Eden-Roc: The deeply private world of Les Cabanes. In these thirty-three cabins, which are set apart from the hotel, guests can enjoy the ultimate in tranquillity and total peace in communion with the mesmerizing enchantment of the sea and the luminous horizon—and Giovanni and his team always in the background, ready to attend to their every need.

Tell us an anecdote: I'm not the person to ask, I'm afraid. Like the three monkeys, I hear no evil, see no evil, and speak no evil.

The best part about your job: Doing everything possible to make guests happy.

The hardest part about your job: Complying with every unusual new request as though it happens all the time.

The skill that encapsulates your professionalism: Carrying a tray.

The tool you can't do without: The telephone.

The sound that tells you all is well: Les Cabanes waking to the chirping of the cicadas.

The most frustrating thing: Capricious requests and the weather.

What do you wear for work? White trousers and a polo shirt.

Would you like to have done a different job? No.

Your most memorable experience with a guest: The exchanges and friendships that grow up over the years.

YOUR MOTTO:

"Live and let live."

Following pages: Giovanni Rizzi, maître d'hôtel, Les Cabanes (left), and Lilian Bonnefoi, head pastry chef, on his way to Les Cabanes.

THE HEAD GARDENER
Angelo Macri

Angelo has devoted virtually his entire working life to the Hôtel du Cap Eden-Roc, where his realm is perhaps the gentlest and greenest of anyone's. As head gardener for nearly twenty-one years, he knows every aspect, every nook and cranny, of the grounds: The tiniest moss or lichen, the blackbirds, the prevailing wind, the scents of the flowers . . .

Tell us an anecdote: I have vivid memories of Bill Cosby. Not just because he was so nice but also because he was so tall. One of his favorite games was to pick us up as he passed and dangle us a meter and a half above the ground! I also remember the visits of Mr. Oetker, the owner. When he was out in the gardens, he would always raise his cap to us, a mark of respect that I always found very touching.

The best part about your job: I love doing everything in the grounds, and I enjoy the variety—pruning, planting, the whole range of jobs.

The hardest part about your job: Trying never to disturb the guests. Instead of mowing the lawn in front of the hotel in the morning, for example, we wait until after lunch when they go to the pool. We have to juggle things all the time.

The skill that encapsulates your professionalism: The secret of good pruning: work fast but not too fast, and cut with confidence.

The tool you can't do without: Pruning shears and my Opinel knife.

The sound that tells you all is well: Birdsong, especially the blackbirds.

The most frustrating thing: In bad weather, the wind and the salt which is carried by the sea spray and which burns the plants.

What do you wear for work? T-shirt (green in summer) and green trousers.

Would you like to have done a different job? When I was younger, I wanted to be a builder, but now I like being a gardener.

A gift you would like to give: Universal happiness.

YOUR MOTTO:

"Be true to yourself, stay grounded."

Preceding pages: Jean-Luc Maïorana, the poolman.
Opposite: Mohamed Boubaker, gardener. Following pages: Jean-Paul Basler, estate pruner.

THE HANDYMAN
Gilles Ricordel

Even in paradise the lightbulbs occasionally need changing. And so for sixteen years, Gilles has tended the hotel's essential systems: Its cables and pipes, the wiring that creates its atmospheric lighting and the plumbing that feeds the white ceramic of its bathrooms.

The best part about your job: Repairing the irreparable.

The hardest part about your job: The heat.

The tool you can't do without: My toolbox.

The sound that tells you all is well: Silence.

What do you wear for work? Trousers and a T-shirt.

Would you like to have done a different job? Yes, I'd like to have lived my dreams!

A gift you like to give: My services.

YOUR MOTTO:

"Egality."

Pages 62-63: Angelo Macri, head gardener (left), and Karim Almssaili, gardener.
Pages 64-65: A team of gardeners working on the hotel's allée d'honneur.
Preceding pages: Christine Vincentelli, florist.

THE PAINTER
Jack Iacomelli

If the Hôtel du Cap Eden-Roc sometimes looks like a painting, it has the talented Jack to thank. For more than twenty years, Jack's paints and brushes have fine-tuned every palette here—perhaps even the blue of the heavens.

The best part about your job: Honing my skills in such a fabulous setting and always having something different to do.

The hardest part about your job: Stupidity (or people watching you).

The skill that encapsulates your professionalism: Careful cutting to give a neat edge (goggles recommended).

The tool you can't do without: A palette knife for clean, sharp edges.

The sound that tells you all is well: Silent approval when my work is finished.

The most frustrating thing: Not going in the same direction.

Your favorite time or place: The beaches at Ramatuelle.

What do you wear for work? If I could choose, Bermuda shorts and a T-shirt.

Would you like to have done a different job? Yes, I'd like to have run a small residential hotel.

Your most memorable experience with a guest: The naturalness of some millionaires who are quite happy to have their photographs taken with members of staff.

A gift you like to give: Perfume.

YOUR MOTTO:

"Always have a goal," or "Keep on keeping on."

THE BARMAN
Anthony Ciacia

After training at the Centre de Formation des Apprentis en Hôtellerie et Restauration in Cannes, Anthony worked at Les Terraillers restaurant in Biot. Twelve years ago he came to work at the Hôtel du Cap Eden-Roc where for the past seven years he has been in charge of the bar.

Tell us an anecdote: Not a day passes without something happening. But the occasion that made the deepest impression on me was when Bruce Willis and Sharon Stone arrived. The bar was pretty busy but when she came in, the earth seemed to come to a stand still. The silence was total. She ordered a tea.

The best part about your job: What I enjoy most is the extraordinary setting, obviously, but also the atmosphere and the sense of team spirit. We all have a close bond with one another and one glance is enough to make the others understand. We work by instinct.

The hardest part about your job: The long hours that we work during the Cannes Film Festival—though we get so caught up in the atmosphere that we lose count of them.

The skill that encapsulates your professionalism: Shaking cocktails. Every barman has his own technique, his own special way of holding the shaker.

The tool you can't do without: The cocktail shaker and mixing glass.

The sound that tells you all is well: When the bar is busy, people are happy and there's a good atmosphere, there's lots of chatting and laughing and drinking of cocktails. Then you know everything is OK.

The most frustrating thing: Nothing much, really—it's not very complicated, except, perhaps, for remembering all the cocktails.

What do you wear for work? Very strict! Black trousers, white shirt, black bow tie, white jacket—like a chef de rang, except that our bow ties are smaller.

Would you like to have done a different job? Not at all. It's great, and you get attached to it. I wouldn't change it for the world!

A gift you like to give: Flowers for my sweetheart.

YOUR MOTTO:

"Be patient! In time, grass turns into milk."

Following pages: Franck Molinaro, chef de rang (left) and Alessandro Coli, 1/2 chef de rang

76

THE MAÎTRE D'HÔTEL, EDEN-ROC PAVILION
Elio Altomari

Born in Italy forty-six years ago, Elio traveled across Europe to learn his trade, working in Germany, England, Switzerland, and Italy before arriving at the Hôtel du Cap Eden-Roc in 1982. Since then he has risen through the ranks, from room service to the dining room and grill before becoming maître d'hôtel in the gourmet restaurant.

Tell us an anecdote: Strangely, we see so many stars and other prominent figures that it all begins to seem quite normal. That said, I'll never forget the fabulous party for Madonna in 1987, with Arnold Schwarzenegger and other celebrities. And there was the concert the Gipsy Kings gave in front of an audience of a couple hundred. That was amazing!

The best part about your job: Dealing with guests and chatting with them. Like them, we look forward to seeing each other every summer. Although they're not really friends, we have something unusual in common: We spend the summer together!

The hardest thing about your job: The hardest thing for me at the moment, if I'm completely honest, is watching my twelve-year-old son grow up!

The skill that encapsulates your professionalism: Everything lies in the way you welcome a guest. That is the crucial moment. You have to make guests feel that we are all there for them while at the same time keeping a proper distance. At such moments you realize that this job is a bit like acting: Our gestures and expressions say it all. They have to be stylized.

The tool you can't do without: A pen and order book, matches, a cigar cutter and of course, a bottle opener.

The sound that tells you all is well: A happy murmur from the tables. When you see someone looking around for you, you know there's something wrong!

The most frustrating thing: No problem is insoluble, except perhaps when different parties arrive together. You have to make sure nobody has to wait too long, which means acting quickly and decisively, without upsetting anyone.

Following pages: *Andrea Delvo, restaurant commis (left), and Mattia Gasperi, 1/2 chef de rang.*

What do you wear for work? Black trousers, white shirt, cream jacket and a mauve tie to match the table settings—and the carpet!

Would you like to have done a different job? No.

Your most memorable experience with a guest: When they tell you as they leave that they've enjoyed a wonderful evening with you.

YOUR MOTTO:

"Honesty."

Opposite: Andrea Zavattari, maître d'hôtel (left), and Alberto Cataldo, restaurant commis.
Following pages: Antoine Belles, purchasing manager (left), and Philippe and Mario Gualerzi, cabinetmakers.

84

THE BAKER
Alex Hyvonnet

Alex has worked for just a year in the hotel's kitchens—where breads, croissants, brioches and *pains aux raisins* are baked fresh daily.

The best part about your job: The opportunity to innovate, which allows me to give free rein to my imagination. There's a huge feeling of satisfaction when people enjoy what I make.

The hardest part about your job: The hours which mean I have to have quite a strict daily routine.

The skill that encapsulates your professionalism: Taking things out of the oven, as that's the moment when I first see the finished item. It's a defining moment for which I have to use a traditional flat wooden shovel with a long handle with dexterity and speed.

The tool you can't do without: That would have to be the dough cutter that I use to lift the dough out of the kneading trough and divide it up. It's known as the baker's third hand.

The sound that tells you all is well: The noise the dough makes as it absorbs the air at the end of kneading. We say it "sings."

Your favorite time or place: A good meal with friends made with local ingredients. I think we often don't pay enough attention to the joy to be had from simple things.

What do you wear for work? Cap, checked trousers and shoes—you would not have any doubt as to what I do for a living.

Would you like to have done a different job? I've never thought about it, I find this one so rewarding.

Your most memorable experience with a guest: A simple compliment on my bread.

A gift you like to give: I like to give decorated bread to people I love and heart-shaped *petits pains* to the one I love.

YOUR MOTTO:
"Do everything with love."

THE SOUS-CHEF
Olivier Gaïatto

Olivier has been a sous-chef in the hotel's kitchens since the summer of 2000. As second-in-command to executive chef Arnaud Poëtte, he is able to oversee the creation of all the dishes and to stand in for him when required.

Tell us an anecdote: Once at a banquet a guest ordered caviar as the appetizer for all his guests, followed—as if it were the most natural thing in the world—by spaghetti *bolognaise.*

The best part about your job: Sharing ideas, communicating a passion for taste and style, always doing your best and making guests happy.

The hardest part about your job: Always keeping up the same rhythm and the highest standards.

The skill that encapsulates your professionalism: For me, there is nothing to equal the way you add the sauce before the plate leaves the kitchen. It's the parting gesture, encapsulating all the love that you have put into the preparation of the plate.

The tool you can't do without: The spoon, as sensual as it is precise.

The sound that tells you all is well: The sizzling of meat, fish, or vegetables as they wait impatiently on a corner of the stove.

Your favorite time or place: The head chef's office when all the chefs and pastry chefs meet after the service to plan suggestions for the following day.

What do you wear for work? Jacket, trousers, and chef's hat.

Would you like to have done a different job? Yes, a cabinetmaker.

Your most memorable experience with a guest: When they come and tell us they've been bowled over by our cuisine.

A gift you like to give: A meal at the new restaurant in Antibes, L'Armoise.

YOUR MOTTO:

"Hold tight and stick together; the storm will pass."

Opposite: Olivier Gaïatto, sous-chef (left), and Arnaud Poëtte, executive chef.
Following pages: The kitchens.

THE PASTRY SOUS-CHEF
Cyril Billaud

For nearly a decade, Cyril has worked in a cloud of confectioner's sugar in the most demanding domain of the hotel's kitchens: One spoonful too much of cream and the gâteau will topple; one too many of sugar and the soufflé will collapse. Whereas savory dishes may be allowed a measure of indulgence or interpretation, *patisserie* demands ruthless precision.

Tell us an anecdote: I'm still moved by the memory of a lady who was determined to cut her own birthday cake. A tiny detail: it was her hundredth birthday.

The best part about your job: What I love most is that every day is different. I'm not confined to making one cake, for example, but instead I can express my passion in many different ways. In addition to desserts, I'm also involved in creating breakfasts, *entremets*, and ice creams.

The hardest part about your job: The most difficult thing in this job is coping with the irregular hours.

The skill that encapsulates your professionalism: Making pastry.

The tool you can't do without: The whip.

The sound that tells you all is well: The humming of our machines.

Your favorite time or place: The canteen.

What do you wear for work? Jacket, trousers, and chef's hat.

Would you like to have done a different job? Yes, if I'd had to do something else, I would have liked to work with nature and animals.

Your most memorable experience with a guest: The Lionel Richie concert at the hotel and the fireworks display afterward.

A gift you like to give: Flowers.

THE HEAD SOMMELIER
Xavier Dinet

Since his recent arrival at the Hôtel du Cap Eden-Roc, this young sommelier has fully embraced the importance of his role: Selecting wines from an outstanding cellar for the mutual benefit of guests and their dinner. A sort of gastronomic ringmaster, he must select the ideal vintage for both the guest's taste and the chef's creation.

Tell us an anecdote: One day last year a vineyard in Burgundy wanted to get in touch with us about an order but wires got crossed, and their call was put through to a guest who happens to have the same name as me. Obviously, he had no memory of having ordered sixty bottles of Meursault! It took ten minutes to work out where the misunderstanding lay. He and I still laugh about it.

The best part about your job: Introducing guests to new wines and seeing their faces light up as they taste them.

The hardest part about your job: The psychology of guests: sometimes it's difficult to work out what they expect or want.

The skill that encapsulates your professionalism: Tasting and decanting the wines.

The tool you can't do without: My sommelier's knife, which enables me to take the cap off neatly and to remove the cork from the bottle.

The sound that tells you all is well: The popping of a Champagne bottle!

Your favorite time or place: A visit to the vineyard or a tasting in the cellar of a gifted vintner.

What do you wear for work? A dark suit.

Would you like to have done a different job? No.

Your most memorable experience with a guest: The occasion when a guest ordered a Euros 12,000 bottle of Hermitage "La Chapelle" 1961 and offered a glass to all the wine staff.

Following pages: Xavier Dinet with Sylvain Herpe and Pierrick Fischer, both commis sommelier.

98

A gift you like to give: Taking people on a tour of different vineyards without leaving the table.

YOUR MOTTO:

"Drink well, stay sober!"

THE ACCOUNTANT
Rosette Parente

Rosette has worked as an accountant, checking figures and characters for clarity, for more than twenty years.

The best part about your job: The contact with people, listening and communicating.

The hardest part about your job: Keeping my concentration up till the end of the day.

The tool you can't do without: My jewelry.

The sound that tells you all is well: Laughter.

The most frustrating thing: This questionnaire!

Your favorite time or place: The sea.

Would you like to have done a different job? Yes, I'd like to have been an actress.

A gift you like to give: Flowers and plants.

YOUR MOTTO:

"Keep a sense of humor."

THE ACCOUNTANT
Stéphanie Bertolino

Since 1997 Stéphanie has occupied a key post at the heart of the hotel's administration: Accountant. Concealed behind a door identical to those leading to guests' rooms is the hive of activity that is her office, housing a staff of five.

Tell us an anecdote: Only the size of some of the bills—but there's nothing anecdotal about them!

The best part about your job: The variety.

The hardest part about your job: Stocktaking.

The tool you can't do without: The computer and calculator.

The sound that tells you all is well: Silence.

Your favorite time or place: Being in the country and also little parties in the photocopying room to celebrate birthdays and the like.

Would you like to have done a different job? Yes, interior design.

Your most memorable experience with a guest: An invitation from a guest to a lovely party every year.

A gift you like to give: My time.

YOUR MOTTO:

"Be discreet,

and do unto others as they would do to you."

The Suppliers

In my time I have seen a hundred artisans,
a hundred labourers, wiser and happier
than University rectors.

MICHEL DE MONTAIGNE, *Essays*

THE OLIVE OIL
Gérard Baussy

For thirty years, the Hôtel du Cap Eden-Roc has bought its olive oil from Gérard Baussy, demonstrating the importance it places upon continuity in its choice of suppliers. Olive oil is a vital thread linking the seasons of the year, a Proustian madeleine of summer in Antibes. Each return here is greeted by the same eternal constants: The heat of the sun, the cool of the shade, the tranquility of the nights, the lapping of the waves—and the aroma of the olive oil.

Tell us an anecdote: One day a guest at the Hôtel du Cap Eden-Roc called the olive mill to ask us to make a delivery of oil to his boat, in the harbor at Antibes. He wanted oil from the same olives that he had sampled in the restaurant of the Eden-Roc Pavilion.

The best part about your job: The pressing of extra-virgin olive oil. There's a tremendous pleasure to be had in smelling the aromas and tasting the new flavors.

The hardest part about your job: The selection of the olives and deciding the right storage time to guarantee the finest quality.

The skill that encapsulates your professionalism: Calculating the malaxation time for the olive paste and the temperature for cold-pressing.

The tool you can't do without: The washing machine that removes all impurities from the olives.

The sound that tells you all is well: The sound of the mill.

The most frustrating thing: Olive stones.

Your favorite time or place: At the mill "la Brissaude": toasted bread rubbed with garlic and drizzled with the new season's oil.

What do you wear for work? Olive green overalls.

Would you like to have done a different job? Yes, a vintner.

Your most memorable experience with a client: The day when a customer told me that the olive oil of the Moulin de Baussy, in the village of Spéracèdes, had been chosen by the *New York Post* as the best olive oil in New York.

A gift you like to give: A little olive tree.

YOUR MOTTO:

"Anything is possible if you truly believe in it."

And the Baussy family motto since 1699: *Sicut Saxum immotus.*

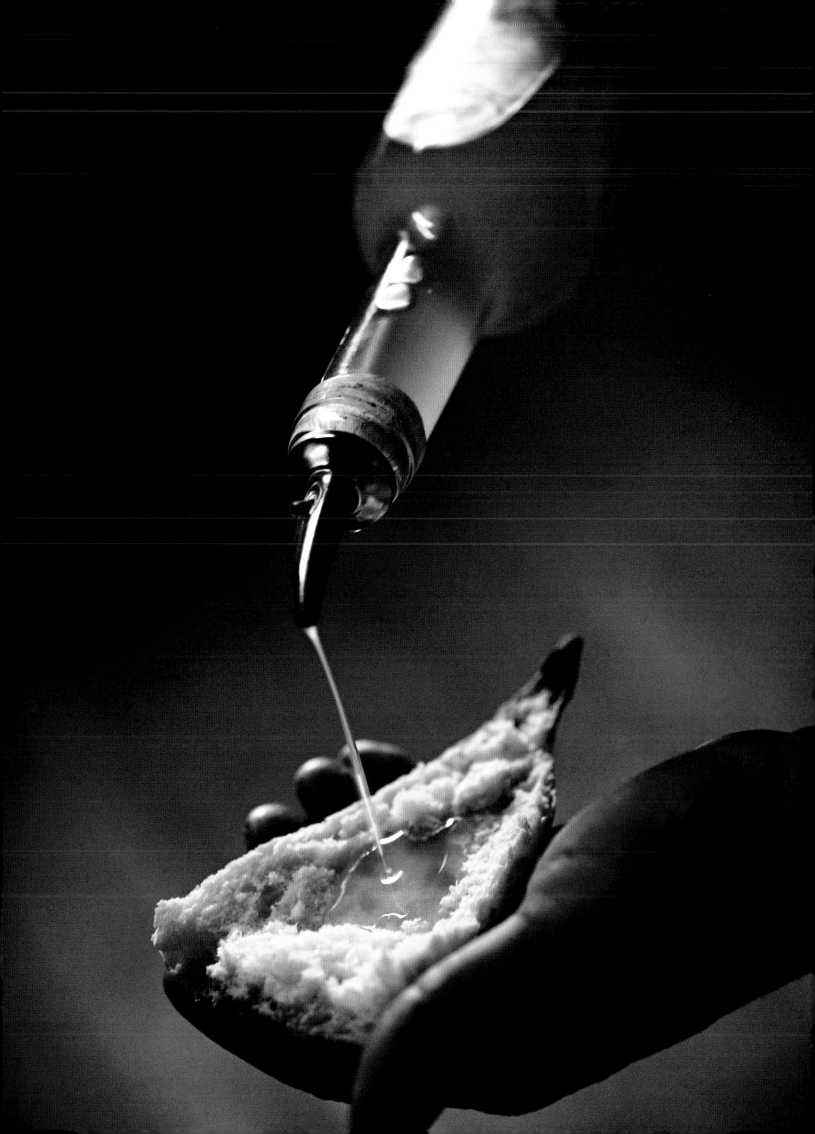

THE WINE
The monks of the Abbaye de Lérins

The most remarkable presence on the Hôtel du Cap Eden-Roc's wine list must surely be the wine produced by the Cistercian monks of the Abbaye de Lérins. The tiny island of Lérins, lying less than a kilometer off the tip of La Croisette in Cannes, enjoys commanding views of the coast from Saint-Tropez to Monaco; to these it owes its fortified monastery, founded in 1050 to defend the mainland against the Saracens.

Tell us an anecdote: The abbey visitors' book contains a message from the poet Paul Claudel dated April 10th, 1936: "Lérins is like a sliver of prayer amid a sea of eternity."

The best part about your job: Our ethical approach to our work and our products involves a commitment to quality and fair trade. The pleasure of work that is well done at every stage guarantees a product of the highest quality and respect for our customers.

The hardest part about your job: The question we ask ourselves is this: How do we go about introducing the products of our monastery into the market economy? That is, into an economic system that at first glance is so incompatible with the underlying values of our lives, devoted as they are to the service of God? How should we respond to competition —too often aggressive—from a consumer society, and to the disturbing exploitation of the image of monastic life by the advertising industry? At the Abbaye de Lérins we have chosen to respond through respect, through being open about who we are and our way of life, and through the quality of our products.

What do you wear for work? Cassock and blue apron.

Your most memorable experience with a client: Undoubtedly, the simple pleasure of anonymous customers. But also the recognition we receive from experts such as Stéphane Thirat, sommelier at L'Arpège restaurant in Paris, who has described our wines' astonishingly deep garnet robe with flashes of violet, its magnificent patina, its dazzling *disque*, its subtle and delicate nose, a hint of hydromel and a few balsamic notes—weighty on the palate but with a smoothness that whisks the wine lover off on a spice-laden odyssey!

YOUR MOTTO:

"Peace and joy."

THE WINE
Henri de Saint Victor of Château de Pibarnon

The wine cellars at the Hôtel du Cap Eden-Roc have for many years been fortunate enough to welcome the vintages of this Provençal wine classified as an Appellation d'Origine Contrôlée Bandol. Not only are they justly celebrated, these are also wines that—embodying as they do a harmonious link between the delights of the table and the surrounding landscape—add an extra dimension to any stay in this favored spot.

The best part about your job: The feeling of creating a luxury product while keeping your feet firmly on the ground—and sometimes your boots in the mud!

The hardest part about your job: The blank incomprehension of some wealthy buyers and "label chasers" who dismiss out of hand all limited-edition crus and are incapable of detecting the finesse, character, grace (and sometimes disgrace) that lend some wines true personality and presence.

The skill that encapsulates your professionalism: In the vineyard, the precise, rapid snip of the shearers as the vintner bends low over the vines to prune them in the depths of winter, and the majestic sweep of the pruning knife as it shears the tips of the young shoots. In the cellar, the exhausting work of punching down the chapeau of grapes by hand, releasing the fine and noble tannins from the skins into the must; the sampling of the wine with a pipette as it ages; and the ensuing judgments as to the work to be done. This is where the vigneron's task really lies: In judging the stage the wine has reached and in extrapolating its future, guiding and correcting it, without at the same time exerting too heavy a hand. Good wine is wine that has aged with a degree of freedom. To exert too much control is to shape it too rigidly; to give it too little guidance, on the other hand, is to abandon your responsibility to it. The tool you can't do without: A good nose and palate!

The sound that tells you all is well: In this arid Mediterranean climate, the rains of spring and autumn; the gurgling of the wines during fermentation, after the harvest, and their sustained rhythm as they continue to age, now alone and in freedom as the cellar seems suddenly to lie dormant; the bell that announces the arrival of wine aficionados for a good tasting and a satisfying exchange of views; the crackling of the open fire with thrushes spit-roasting on it, with a magnum of the 1995 ready to accompany them.

The most frustrating thing: The weather. Every year at harvest time it's the weather that makes us improvise. Like the cast of a stage musical, we all have our lines and the score at the tips of our fingers, everyone is in their place, everything has been rehearsed a hundred times, but we don't know what the audience or the venue will be like. Whatever happens, the *terroir* is a constant, the *terroir* is the score. Add to this the aridity of the climate and the power of the land, which are at once our staunchest allies and our strongest catalyst . . . It is this combination of summer drought and winter mildness that creates the complexities of our wines, their power and strength of personality, tempered and deepened by their softness and elegance.

Your favorite time or place: Harvest lunch in the orangery at the château.

What do you wear for work? Stout jeans and shoes for working in the vineyards, a good shirt to add a note of style, and, for the sheer pleasure of it, a jacket in reserve, ready for the next invitation to a blind tasting of Pibarnon and other great wines.

Would you like to have done a different job? I love the sea, and I'm very competitive, so I could see myself competing in regattas, but making wine is so much closer to the land, so much more sensuous, that it brings me more satisfaction than I could ever have hoped for. The only thing is that it's a labor of love that only begins to reap rewards once you're well into your thirties. I'm forty-four, so I can begin to breathe a sigh of relief!

Your most memorable experience with a client: The day when a tasting in the cellar led to lunch, followed by a whole afternoon at the château, and culminated in a dinner where we set the world to rights to the accompaniment of some extremely fine wines (and not just Pibarnons: I also opened some of my best "swaps".

A gift you like to give: My latest *coup de coeur*, such as a Grange des Pères 2002, an Ibérico de Bellota ham brought back from Madrid, a live lobster bought from the tank at Ploubazlanec, or a fishing trip on my boat for sea urchins, accompanied by a 2007 rosé.

YOUR MOTTO:
"No doctrine is so profound that it can't be understood
with three glasses of good wine."

*Opposite: Comte and Comtesse de Saint Victor
with their son Éric.*

THE CHEESE
Gilles Ceneri

Although not all guests may avail themselves of its pleasures (rather like the pool), an excellent cheese board is an indispensable badge of honor for any establishment of quality. Casting admiring glances at it as it sails past them, now and then guests permit themselves to delve into its treasures. All the more reason why, on that day of all days, every appellation should be at the peak of ripeness! This is where Gilles Ceneri, famous throughout the Riviera, comes in, keeping a watchful eye over his cheeses, cosseting and maturing them until that fateful day when the waiter will indicate the one to which a guest's fancy inclines.

The best part about your job: Discovering new cheeses and learning to understand the way in which they age in the cellars, from maturity to the table.

The skill that encapsulates your professionalism: Caressing the cheese.

The tool you can't do without: The wire butter slicer.

The sound that tells you all is well: Water dripping onto stainless-steel sheets to keep the cellars damp.

Your favorite time or place: Breakfast time, with coffee, a baguette and a cheese that's been left on one of the shelves.

What do you wear for work? White coat, apron, cap and boots.

Your most memorable experience with a client: Being the third generation, I don't yet have the distance necessary to appreciate such moments but simply feeling the beginnings of a friendship forming is very special to me.

A gift you like to give: A cheese board.

YOUR MOTTO:

"The world belongs to early risers."

A tribute to M. Édouard Ceneri.

THE GOAT CHEESE
Geneviève François & Daniel Georges

In the village of Rocbaron, Geneviève François and Daniel Georges have learned to wait on nature, to watch it in contemplation as the seasons unfold. They make their own goat cheese from start to finish, keeping the Hôtel du Cap Eden-Roc supplied with their famous little *fromages de chèvre de Banne*.

The best part about your job: Being close to the animals. I try to make them happy. I love going out with my goats and my dogs.

The hardest part about your job: The saddest thing is when a goat is sick. And when they give birth it's very tough both for them and for us

The skill that encapsulates your professionalism: Milking is a delicate task, requiring a genuine feel for it and absolute concentration. Another lovely and very important gesture is the molding of the cheeses with the ladle.

The tool you can't do without: The milk churn and ladle!

The sound that tells you all is well: The cock crowing in the morning and the soothing tinkling of the goats' bells.

The most frustrating thing: A tempting branch that's just out of the goats' reach; the dogs nipping their legs.

Your favorite time or place: When, amid nature's silence, a goat comes to be stroked.

Would you like to have done a different job? No.

Your most memorable experience with a client: Gaining recognition from a major establishment like the Hôtel du Cap Eden-Roc.

A gift you like to give: Farmhouse cheeses.

YOUR MOTTO :

"All's quiet, all's well."

THE WILD STRAWBERRIES
Marie Ange Van Severen

After rich and rewarding professional careers, Marie Ange Van Severen and her spouse, Yves, are now to be found cultivating wild strawberries among the back gardens of Villeneuve-Loubet. There they devote themselves to agriculture with equal measures of determination and a happiness that is both simple and transparent. Working in hot sunshine or cool breezes, they cultivate their Mara des Bois strawberries without soil, avoiding the use of troublesome chemicals and producing yields of mouthwatering perfume and flavor. The fragile fruits are delivered daily to the kitchens of the Hôtel du Cap Eden-Roc where beguiling care is lavished upon them until they are enjoyed with equally beguiling insouciance. Madonna loves them with her cappuccino.

The best part about your job: Being a supplier to such prestigious clients is very gratifying.

The hardest part about your job: Maintaining the regularity of supplies required by our clients.

The skill that encapsulates your professionalism: Calculating the right amount of fertilizer, and above all picking the fruit, twisting them between your thumb and two fingers without pulling them from the plant.

The tool you can't do without: The irrigation time switch.

The sound that tells you all is well: The call of magpies as they fly off when the cat chases them. Magpies are the enemy of strawberry and raspberry growers!

The most frustrating thing: Anthracnosis, a persistent fungus that eats into the crop.

Your favorite time or place: The happy atmosphere as we sort and weigh the day's crop.

What do you wear for work? Boots, sometimes waterproof overalls.

Would you like to have done a different job? No.

A gift you like to give: A pot of jam.

THE VEGETABLES
Aimé Pellegrin

For the past fifteen years, this market gardener in Grasse has risen at dawn to deliver his dewy, fresh vegetables to the Hôtel du Cap Eden-Roc. Pampered and scrutinized for their appearance and quality, they are picked at the peak of perfection.

Tell us an anecdote: I have to confess that I'm rather proud of the fact that I was "discovered" in another restaurant. When one day by chance the current executive chef of the Hôtel du Cap Eden-Roc, Arnaud Poëtte, tasted my asparagus, he got in touch straight away to ask us to deliver to him.

The best part about your job: Watching the vegetables grow.

The hardest part about your job: No question about it: knowing how to handle the vegetables and protect them from insect parasites without interfering too much with their normal, healthy development.

The skill that encapsulates your professionalism: I can't boil it down to one! Growing our vegetables requires a wide range of equipment and many, many hours of work.

What do you wear for work? Shorts, a T-shirt, and, in the summer, bare feet.

Your most memorable experience with a client: That's easy: Knowing that Hollywood stars eat my asparagus!

A gift you like to give: For friends, a basket of freshly picked vegetables.

YOUR MOTTO:

"Work your hardest to create the finest products."

THE COFFEE
Mesdames Sappe & Fauchet

For many years—indeed, "forever"—the Antibes merchant Négus Blanc has supplied the Hôtel du Cap Eden-Roc with its coffee. Every bean has been roasted in the *rotisseries* of this Riviera institution.

Tell us an anecdote: The former owner of the Hôtel du Cap Eden-Roc, Monsieur Sella, used to love coming into the shop. He shared a passion for fishing with our father and they used to swap tips about conditions in the shallows off Antibes.

The best part about your job: It's very simple: The best feeling for us is seeing our clients come back.

The hardest part about your job: Constantly keeping up with our clients' changing tastes and requirements.

The tool you can't do without: The coffee roaster.

The sound that tells you all is well: The cracking of the coffee beans as they fall into the cooler, giving off that roasted aroma.

What do you wear for work? Nothing special, just smart casual.

Would you like to have done a different job? No, I've grown up with an understanding and love of this job.

Your most memorable experience with a client: The pleasure we get from clients' enjoyment of our decor, with its evocative aromas and colors, and its memories of travel and childhood.

A gift you like to give: A new variety of coffee!

YOUR MOTTO:

"To develop and improve every day."

THE PRINTING
Jacques Fantino

The relationship between Jacques Fantino and the Hôtel du Cap Eden-Roc stretches back many years as Jacques's grandfather used to work for Monsieur Sella, the hotel's former owner. The history of the printing house goes back even further, to 1868. Here, in other words, many a line of type—whether condensed, copperplate or roman—has told many a story. There is no corner of the hotel that has not been graced by the consonants and vowels of the Imprimerie Fantino. 140 years later, Jacques Fantino has recently earned the right to use the Imprim'Vert logo guaranteeing stringent standards of recycling and environmentalism.

Tell us an anecdote: When I was a student, I worked as a doorman at the hotel under Michel Babin de Lignac (known as "Le Comte"). On the last day of the season, my friends who worked around the pool had the bright idea of throwing me into the pool, fully dressed in my uniform. The place was packed and as I dragged myself out of the water in my smart white trousers, the guests who were watching—including Shirley MacLaine and Madame Daniel Hechter—roared with laughter. It was so embarrassing! Fortunately, the manager never got to hear about it.

The best part about your job: Dealing with good customers, the variety of the work, the problems that push you to the highest standards.

The hardest part about your job: Working against the clock.

The skill that encapsulates your professionalism: I love the clatter of a Heidelberg press as the type form is brought up against the frame. This noise was the sound track to my childhood as I used to love watching the printers at work on their machines.

The tool you can't do without: The linen tester, or printer's loupe, an essential gauge of our work.

The sound that tells you all is well: The humming of the four-color machine: it greets me every morning as I come down the little passageway from the Old Town.

Following pages: The team at the Fantino printing works.

The most frustrating thing: Paper that's too stiff or too sensitive to changes of temperature, poor-quality envelopes and ink that just refuses to dry.

Your favorite time or place: Drinks in the workshop with my colleagues, parents, wife and children; our traditional Christmas dinner with the staff; a picnic at sunset on the beach at Les Ondes.

What do you wear for work? My grandfather manned his guillotine in a gray coat, my father his Heidelberg press in blue overalls. Nowadays we wear a serviceable old sweatshirt.

Would you like to have done a different job? I love my work! But I wouldn't have minded being an architect.

Your most memorable experience with a client: Every New Year, I try to design an original greeting card with a theme related to Antibes, and every year I'm impatient to hear the verdict of a faithful customer who always phones me as soon as he receives it.

A gift you like to give: I love giving surprise gifts to my wife and children but I manage to let the cat out of the bag every time.

YOUR MOTTO:

"Spoil yourself!"

Acknowledgments

Philippe Perd, the Hôtel du Cap Eden-Roc Managing Director, and Laurent Vanhoegaerden, the Hôtel du Cap Eden-Roc Resident Manager, wish to thank the monks of the Abbaye de Lérins, Gérard Baussy, Gilles Ceneri, Jacques Fantino, Geneviève François & Daniel Georges, Aimé Pellegrin, Henri de Saint Victor, mesdames Sappe & Fauchet, Marie Ange Van Severen as well as Jean-Michel Sordello, Brice Kemper and Patricia Guillot.

The Publisher would like to thank Philippe Perd, the Hôtel du Cap Eden-Roc Managing Director as well as Jean-Michel Sordello and Laurent Vanhoegaerden.